200 TIPS FOR KITCHENS & BATHROOMS

200 TIPS FOR KITCHENS & BATHROOMS

Xavier Torras Isla

FIREFLY BOOKS

A Firefly Book

Published by Firefly Books Ltd. 2012

First printing

Publisher Cataloging-in-Publication Data (U.S.)

Isla, Xavier Torras.
200 tips for kitchens and bathrooms / Xavier Torras Isla.
[800] p. : col. photos. ; cm.
includes index
ISBN-13: 978-1-77085-089-7
1. Kitchens--Design and construction. 2. Bathrooms--Design and construction. I. Title
747.797   dc23   NK2117.K5.1853 2012

Library and Archives Canada Cataloguing in Publication

A CIP record for this title is available from Library and Archives Canada

Published in the United States by
Firefly Books (U.S.) Inc.
P.O. Box 1338, Ellicott Station
Buffalo, New York 14205

Published in Canada by
Firefly Books Ltd.
66 Leek Crescent
Richmond Hill, Ontario L4B 1H1

Cover design: Erin R. Holmes/Soplari Design

Printed in China

This book was developed by:
LOFT Publications, S.L.
Via Laietana, 32, 4º, of. 92
08003 Barcelona, Spain

Editorial coordinator: Aitana Lleonart
Editor: Àlex Sánchez Vidiella
Texts: Xavier Torras Isla
Art director: Mireia Casanovas Soley
Design and layout coordination: Claudia Martínez Alonso
Layout: Cristina Simó, Yolanda G. Román
Layout assistant: Kseniya Palvinskaya

Cover image credits
Front: © Mitchell Barutha
Spine: © Lisa Turay
Back: © John Keith; (from L to R): © Scavolini; © Darren Chung; © Mark Breck; © Darren Chung

INTRODUCTION

When designing a home, people typically focus on areas like the living room, dining room, master bedroom or foyer. These are spaces that are often allotted more than their fair share of square footage, and are considered highlights for visitors to see.

For a long time, kitchens and bathrooms were sidelined when it came to interior design. As rooms with specific functions and necessary practicality, they were relegated to the background. The kitchen was where the work of prepping and cooking was done, and the dining room was where the end result of the feast was presented. Bathrooms were totally private and fully enclosed, keeping what needed to be kept behind closed doors behind those doors.

Fortunately this traditional idea, which excluded kitchens and bathrooms from the beauty, elegance and comfort found elsewhere in the home, has faded. Many factors have contributed to the change, including new needs, new materials, new designers, new technology and even new home styles. The result is that kitchens and bathrooms now have a revered place in the design of a home and have even become some of the most pampered spaces. Homeowners themselves know that these are spaces that are must-use areas, often more important than other rooms both for themselves and when used by guests.

The ideas that have adapted kitchens and bathrooms to their current, updated design are endless. This book attempts to show a variety of different approaches currently used to design or redesign these rooms.

One of the greatest changes found throughout this book is the way that boundaries within the house have changed, in terms of actual walls or the functions of the room. So bathrooms can be integrated with bedrooms and kitchens with dining rooms. This book also reveals how cohesive design can achieve continuity throughout the home, how practicality can combine with luxury, and how old, new, urban and rural features can all combine harmoniously. Most important, we discover that kitchens and bathrooms can reflect our personality the same way as the rest of the rooms in our home.

KITCHENS

LACQUER | STAINLESS STEEL | WOOD | MISCELLANEOUS

LACQUER

When lacquer is given the starring role in a kitchen, it opens up a world of possibilities. Lacquered surfaces are easy to clean, come in a variety of colors and provide an added luminosity to the room.

Lacquer is popular with modular kitchen designs, creating a functional space with an urban feel. Combined with good lighting, the intensity of color that lacquer can provide adds life to a room.

1 The blue cabinets, red wall, green ceiling and white stools delineate this kitchen, while working in harmony with the metal and wood elements. Natural light from the courtyard and the bright fluorescent cylinders amplify these features.

This white Corian countertop doubles as a table, making maximum use of limited space. The side of the wooden cabinetry defines the short hallway leading to the living room.

2

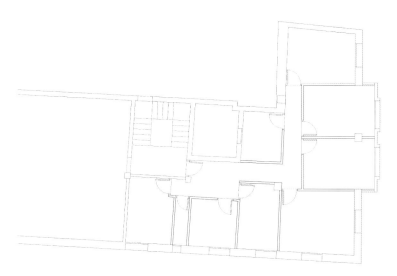

Original floor plan

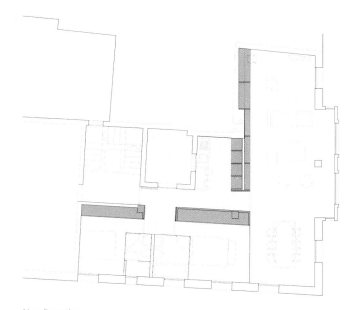

New floor plan

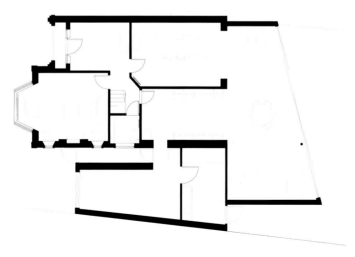

Ground floor plan

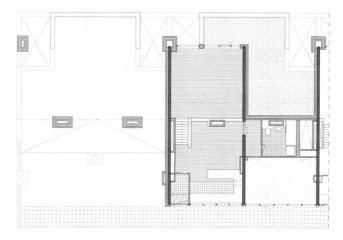

Original floor plan

New floor plan

This kitchen is the epitome of minimalism: pure white, straight lines and very little flourish. The glass table and exterior glass walls give an open, airy and lightweight feel to the space.

3

4 A plain island comprised of a simple sink and faucet and smooth countertop stands between a modular cabinet and the stairwell. The monotone, curved back wall further enhances the presence of this solemn and solid piece.

The kitchen and dining room
flow into one another thanks
to the use of this continuous
white countertop, which can also
be used for activities such as
studying or working. The windows
provide natural light and a
tranquil view.

5

6

Just past the living room threshold are three long rectangular elements: the kitchen workspace, the central island and the old wooden table. This arrangement creates a stylized, linear space.

Here cooking and eating have expanded beyond a more private, traditional enclosure to an inviting space that can even be enjoyed with neighbors. The open design with ample shelving and cabinetry more than compensates for the loss of wall space.

7

8 When you have a large space to work with, it's best used by incorporating sizable furniture, cabinetry and design elements with well-defined work and seating areas along with ample room for traffic flow.

All kitchen equipment, appliances and cabinets extend across one continuous wall, with the central table providing an additional work surface. The white lacquer is accented by the wooden floors and sloped ceiling.

9

10

The central work table divides the space into two areas: the kitchen and the dining room. This division is accentuated further by the predominant material in each space; i.e., wood in the dining area and white lacquer in the kitchen.

11

This open-plan kitchen, characterized by predominantly white elements, connects to the dining area by the continuous wooden floor. Straight, sharp lines and contours further define the overall space.

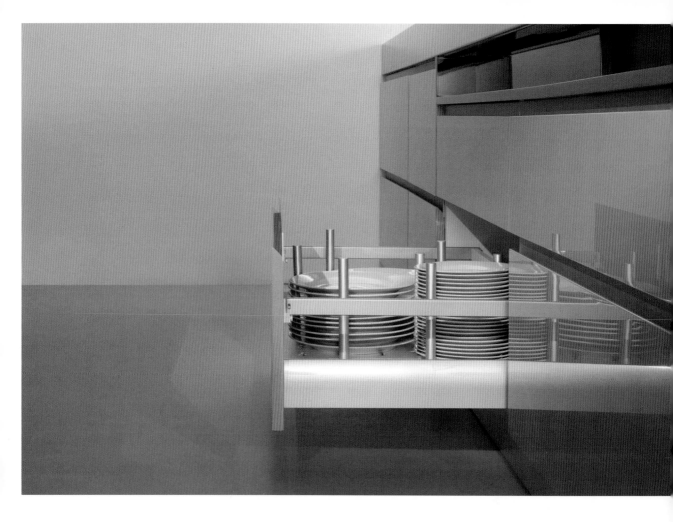

This well-designed kitchen workspace provides storage for plates, as well as other necessary kitchen items. The walls are bare, devoid of high cabinets and shelves, enhancing the clean feel and simplicity of the room.

12

13

The elegant contrast of black and white in this Italian kitchen design is reminiscent of a stylish tuxedo. The contemporary modular feel marries well with classic details like the chandelier.

This kitchen's compact design makes maximum use of space with minimal square footage. The central unit is easy to clean and fully accessible from all sides, with a recessed base that gives a lightweight "floating" effect.

14

15

Being able to access the island from all sides is beneficial, allowing an orderly flow in the space and making cleaning an easy task. Colorful matte hotplates are reflected in the shiny, mirrorlike floor, adding to the lightweight feel in the room.

This kitchen is both functional and sculptural. The asymmetry of the unit, as well as its elevation above the floor, gives it a lightweight, almost cloudlike feel. The monotone coloration, delicate lines and overhead lighting accentuate this unique piece.

16

17 Structural components that can be hidden help maximize the openness and functionality of any kitchen. Here, cabinetry and stairs can be brought out or put away as needed.

18

The curved cooking area is the king of this kitchen, which replicates the look of a modern, pop-themed bar. The workspace allows for full visibility of the fun, colorful dining area.

In this kitchen, the bright red
upper cabinetry is offset by more
subdued white base cabinets.
These modular L-shaped
elements contrast with softer
lines in the dining area.

19

STAINLESS STEEL

The use of stainless steel in the kitchen evokes a contemporary industrial and professional esthetic. However, its quality and strength, along with its clean, practical nature, makes it an intelligent choice for many kitchen designs. Gone are the days when stainless steel was only used for household appliances. The smoothness and luster of metal surfaces brings simplicity and a modern feeling to diverse elements including cabinets, chairs, tables and countertops.

20

The combination of stainless steel appliances with black granite countertops is particulary attractive in this kitchen. Both add a reflective quality to the other elements in the space, providing depth and substance to the overall effect.

The entire set of cabinets and appliances are made of a light-tone stainless steel. Placing the cabinetry against a white wall fully integrates them into the space, almost as if they are embossed.

21

22 Stainless steel works well with a variety of different materials. In this predominantly white kitchen, the countertops, range hood and other metal elements elicit a subtle sense of strength into the design.

23 Small detailed elements (even those hidden at first glance) can be distinguished through the use of stainless steel. The compartments in this drawer are esthetically pleasing and also provide practical and effective storage, keeping food fresh and odor absorption to a minimum.

24

This stainless steel kitchen feels lightweight despite the strength and solidity of the metal. The graceful curve of the workspace is repeated in the cooktop and range hood.

Fans and range hoods are now designed for more than just their practical use to vent out smoke, vapor and odors. This stylish titanium hood hangs at an oblique angle and its mirrorlike quality helps reflect light in the space.

25

26

The highlight of this modern kitchen is the shiny, satin-finish stainless steel range hood, which appears to hover over the cooking area. Its stand-out futuristic design gives it the feel of a work of art.

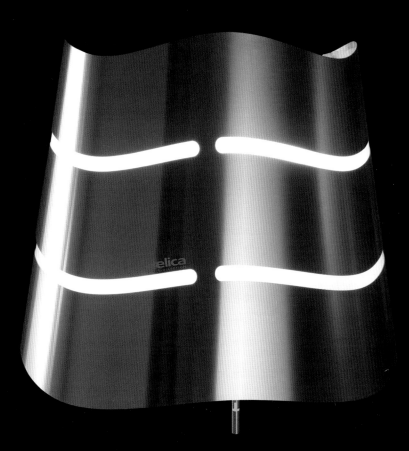

27

The stainless steel tray on this unit provides an industrial feel, and also an air of cleanliness and practicality. Its smooth, polished texture and elevated position help it to stand out against the matte base structure.

28 This island is topped with two stainless steel structures that tower over the compact base: the large sink, which can also be used as a countertop, and the hood. The different levels add to the multidimensional feel of the kitchen.

Here, the countertop hotplate incorporates a dish drying area into the design, while the overhead element contains practical storage compartments. The shiny metal improves light reflection in the space.

29

30

This space contains both kitchen and dining room, but each is delineated by the use of different materials: stainless steel and wood, respectively. The metal used in this compact kitchen reflects the surrounding colors.

This faucet design originated in professional kitchens, but makes a practical addition to the household kitchen. Its swivel arm makes it easy to fill pots without lifting them, and it can be compactly folded up against the wall.

31

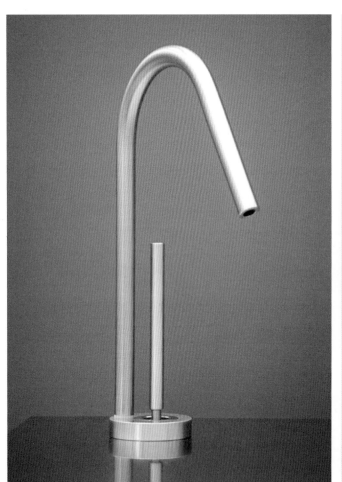
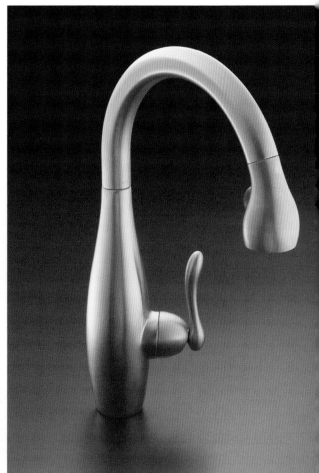

32   This unit adds interest and
      functionality to the kitchen,
      whether used independently or
      integrated into a larger design.
      Featuring full 360-degree
      rotation, its multifunction
      capability creates an area where
      you can prepare, cook and eat.

33 This kitchen unit has an ethereal quality with its gently curved shape, semi-transparent doors and minimalist stainless steel lines.

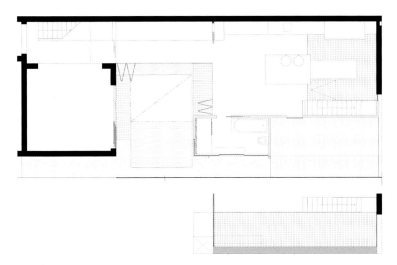

Floor plan

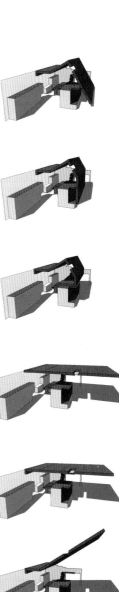

Diagrams

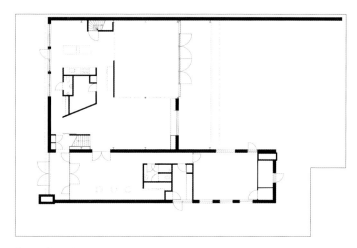

Ground floor plan

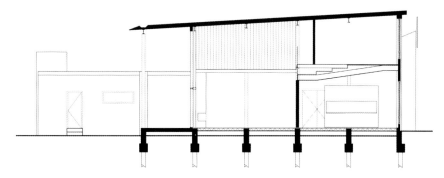

Section

34

This kitchen design is both functional and elegant. In combination, the stainless steel and Corian elements create a strong, urban effect.

Stainless steel distinguishes
this kitchen – in particular, by
identifying the room's appliances –
and stands out against the Corian,
white cabinets and wood parquet
flooring. The shiny metal surfaces
help reflect the sunlight entering
the room.

35

Sketch

36   This pragmatic kitchen design is a good example of the commercial kitchen idea brought to home. The stainless steel island, which matches the appliances, is portable and multifunctional, serving as a table, countertop and storage area.

WOOD

Wood gives a kitchen warmth and a natural feel that no other material can. It comes in a range of shades and textures, all inspirational in the home, either through the smoothness that a polished or varnished surface transmits, or the rustic style that wood creates.

Pillars, exposed beams or wooden floorboards are surfaces that can sometimes be refinished to great beauty, and are great elements that bring interest to kitchen design.

37 Wood dominates in this U-shaped kitchen, which contains ample drawers and cabinetry. Metal accents in the appliances and range hood work well with the tones in the countertop and backsplash.

38

The off-white wooden cabinetry and finishes give this kitchen a luxurious air. The sleek chairs, lightly patterned backsplash and trio of chandeliers complement the room's decor.

39   This kitchen, with its two-tone design and soft yellow door fronts, evokes the feel of a study or workspace. The windows offer a relaxing view of the outdoors and let in ample natural light.

This kitchen harmoniously combines wood, terracotta and stainless steel into a practical and beautiful design. There is a careful attention to detail that contributes to the harmony of the elements.

40

41

The wooden furniture, flooring and beams have been simply finished to retain an unpolished, natural feel. This rustic kitchen is large and warm enough to also be used as a dining room.

Light tones of wood and stone combine in this space, blending in with the natural coastal environment where the home is situated. The large doorway lets in ample light and fresh air.

42

43 The twilight-colored lacquered kitchen contrasts with the warmth of the wood that completes the room. The mirrorlike black surfaces reflect the natural wood elements and strike a counterbalance to the natural materials.

This unit is deceiving, appearing to be a near-solid block featuring a rich range of ochers and browns. Upon closer examination, it reveals a functional kitchen, with concealed storage areas and other practical details.

44

45

This contemporary kitchen combines polished wood and white lacquer. Both areas are subtly reflective, and the long length of cabinetry produces the near-appearance of a continuous back wall.

46 The wood on the island countertop shares the dark brown color of the floor, creating a harmonious effect and exemplifying the warmth of the material. The remaining light-colored cabinetry creates a pleasing contrast.

47 This long, rectangular kitchen is distributed over several parallel work surfaces that combine a variety of different materials. Wood is used in the back-wall work area as well as the kitchen bar.

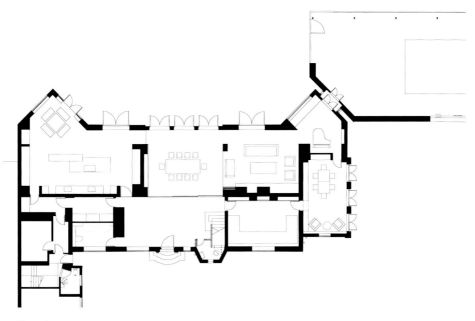

Floor plan

48 The wood in this kitchen produces a warm, homey feel, and complements the darker toned wood on the adjacent dining room floor.

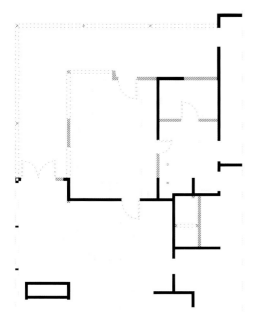

Original floor plan

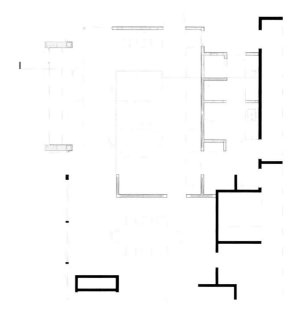

New floor plan

49

Elements of this kitchen, such as the countertop and stainless steel appliances, are designed to either match or effectively contrast the warmth of the wood found here.

50

Sunlight that enters through the tall windows is reflected on a gleaming oak floor, which provides a pleasant light, without reducing privacy in the room. At night, several potlights meet this function.

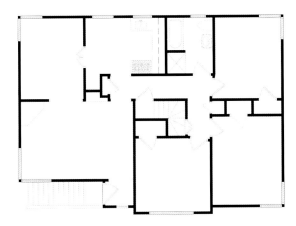

Original floor plan

New floor plan

51 The dark polished wood adds elegance to this kitchen and gives it a contemporary flair. The countertop and dining room table, though made with different materials, effectively share a similar texture.

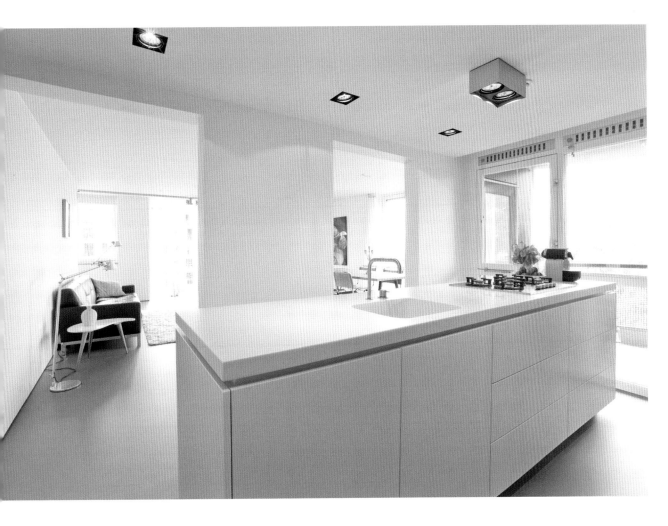

52 The kitchen was placed in an area of the home that links with the rest of the house. The drywall panels create a partial division, but also allow a visual relationship with the adjoining areas.

53 Ceiling-height oak plywood cabinets, devoid of ornamentation or knobs, lie opposite the white Corian island. The continuous, smooth cabinetry finish creates clean lines in the kitchen.

Colors are clear and distinct in this kitchen, integrating the entire space. The wood provides a warm and cosy feel. The placement of furniture and cabinetry creates simultaneous privacy and a visual connection with adjoining areas.

54

Floor plan

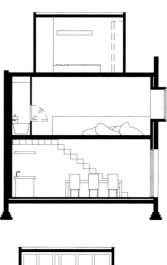

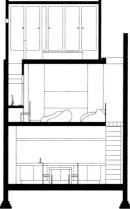

Sections

55   Wood is the main material used in this combined kitchen and dining room. The wood finishes found in the ceiling and steps are repeated in the countertop and book case. Plaster and bricks also contribute to creating the natural boundaries found in the space.

MISCELLANEOUS

Whether there is ample room or limited space, clever design can create brilliant solutions. There are so many ways to be creative: by diffusing boundaries between rooms, complementing existing functions or using materials in an innovative way.

Another way to create ingenious designs is by creating compact units or using hideaway components.

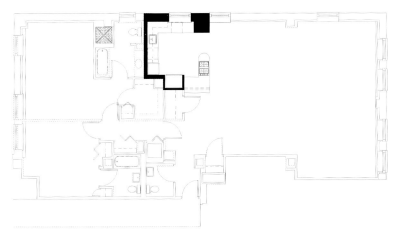

Before renovation plan

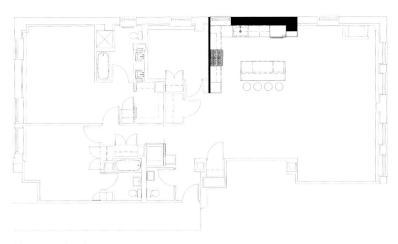

After renovation plan

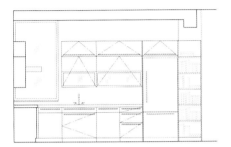
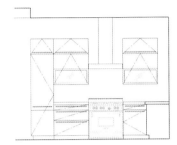
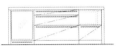

After renovation sections

56

The Calacatta marble used to make these countertops and the island provide a majesty that eases the transition between the kitchen and dining room. The snowy white elements emphasize the distinct design of this space.

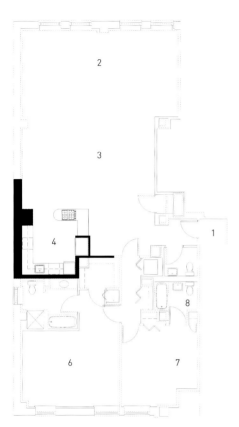

Before renovation plan

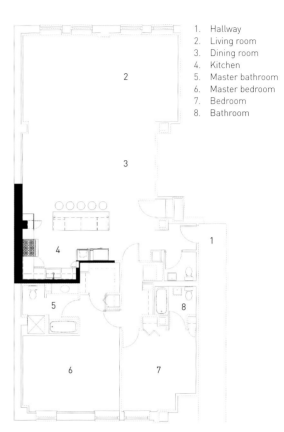

After renovation plan

1. Hallway
2. Living room
3. Dining room
4. Kitchen
5. Master bathroom
6. Master bedroom
7. Bedroom
8. Bathroom

57

An amalgam of colors, textures, materials, shapes and reflections combine in this kitchen and dining room, resulting in an inviting and harmonious effect.

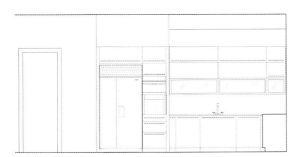
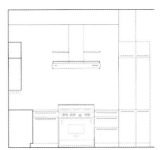

After renovation sections

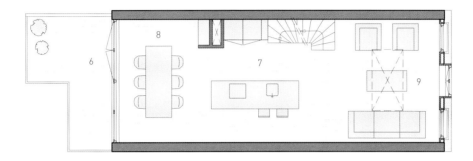

Floor plans

1. Hall
2. Bedroom
3. Study
4. Bathroom
5. Bathroom
6. Terrace
7. Kitchen
8. Dining room
9. Living Room

58 The white and red Corian island plays an important role, acting as the division between the living room and dining room. The predominantly white decor and sleek design give the space an ultra-modern, space-age feel.

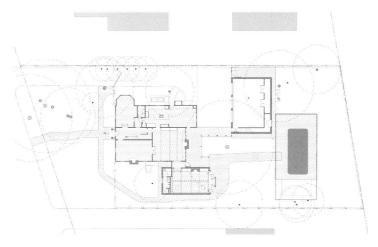

Existing first floor plan

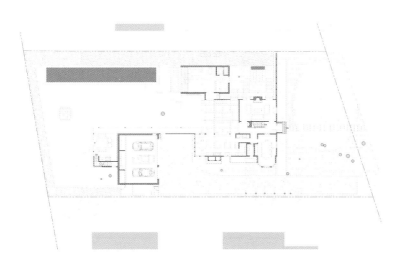

New first floor plan

59 The placement of the windows distributes the natural light over an area that includes stainless steel equipment and lacquered and polished wood storage areas. The result is a pleasing balance between traditional and modern details.

Before plan

After plan

60

The huge windows in this kitchen help integrate it with the natural surroundings found beyond them. In essence, the kitchen becomes part of the landscape.

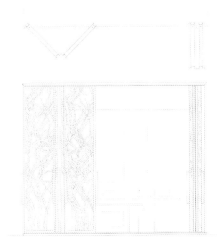

Elevation

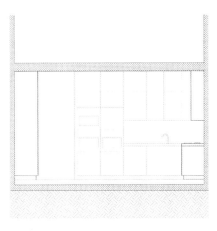

Cross section

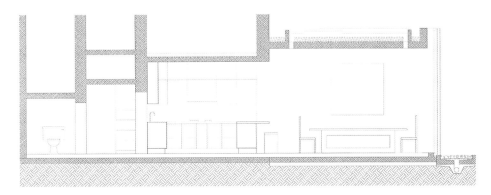

Longitudinal section

61

The outdoor environment is both visibly and physically accessible from this space. The unit perpendicular to the wall doubles as a countertop for the kitchen and an eating area for the dining room.

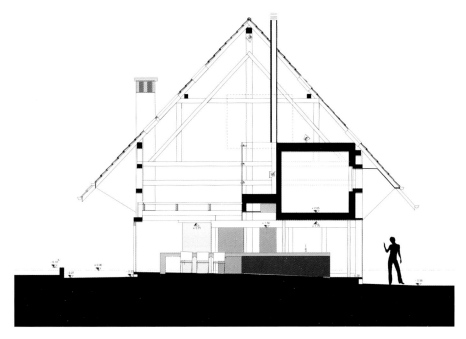

Section

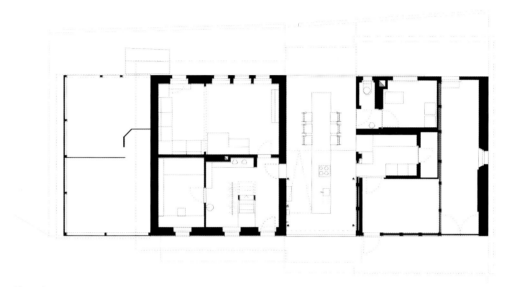

Floor plan

62

This old barn contains a huge, strong table capable of accommodating both cooking activities and meal time. The vivid colors, iron beams and rustic wood seem to naturally integrate.

63

Here, a solid wall separates the kitchen from the living room, but the complementary use of materials and colors pulls the entire room together. In particular, the wood flooring helps unify the space.

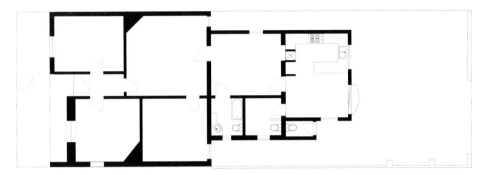

Original floor plan

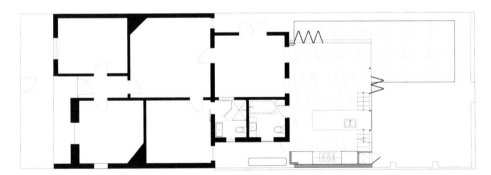

New floor plan

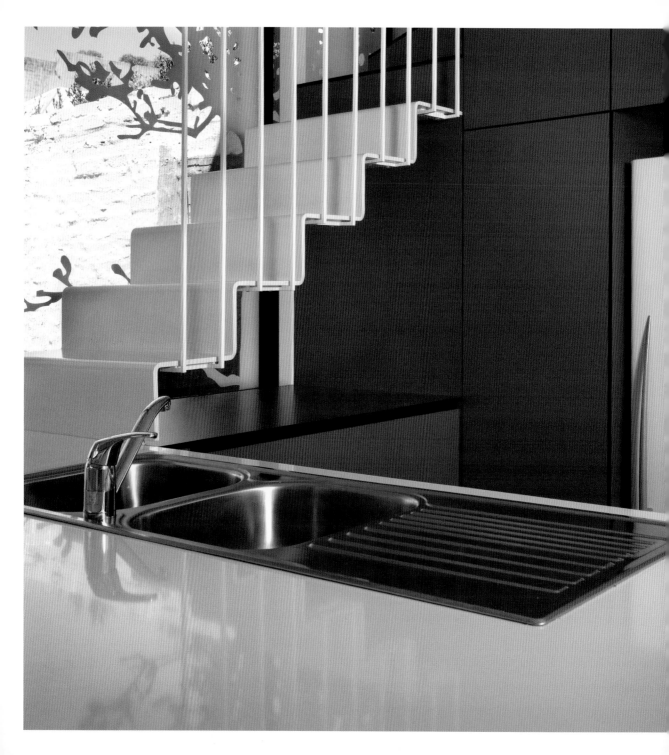

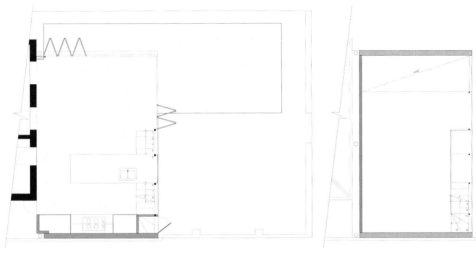

Ground floor plan

Mezzanine

64

The stairs here are reminiscent of folded paper, and turn the kitchen island into part of the staircase. This creates a multidimensional effect in the space.

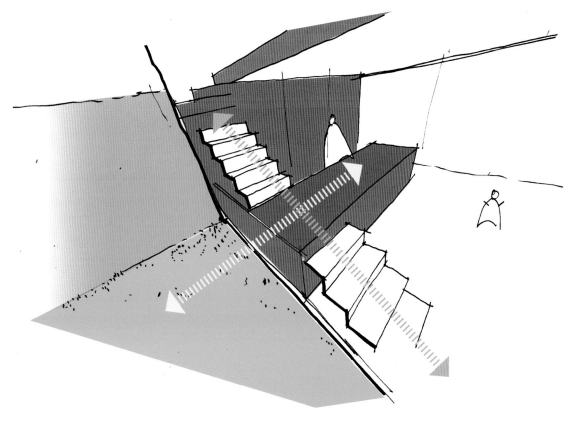

Sketch

The lacquered island, complete with a stainless steel top, helps direct the flow in this kitchen. The reflective surfaces enhance the open, airy space.

65

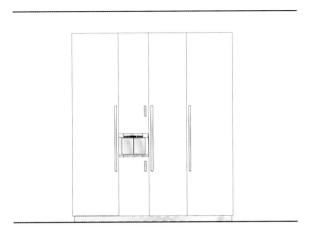

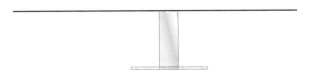

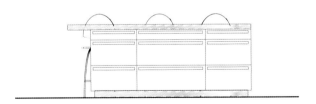

Elevations

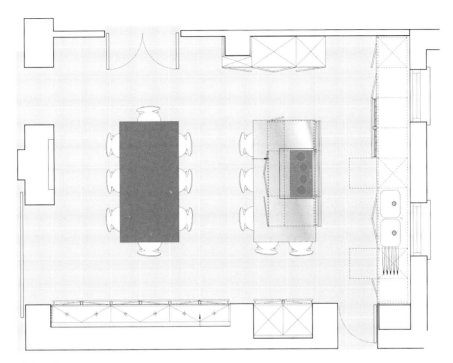

Kitchen plan

66

In harmony with the overall balance of the space, the island has a cooking area on one side and a work surface on the other. Combine this with modern stools, and it becomes an inviting kitchen bar.

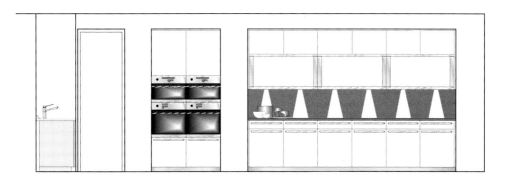

Elevations

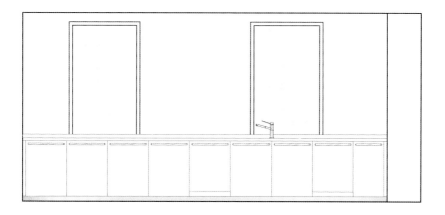

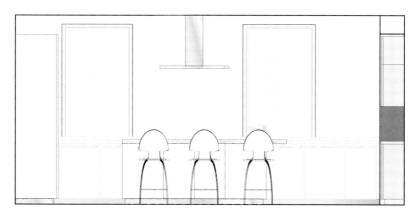

Elevations

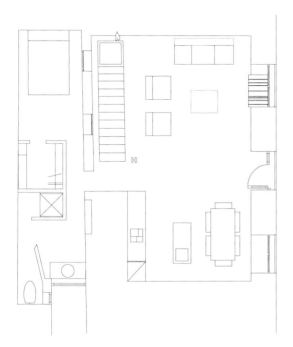
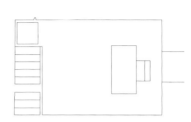

Floor plan

67 A natural and industrial feel combine in this space through the use of feng shui principles and careful attention to the chosen materials.

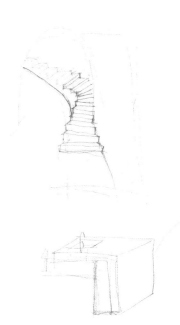

Sketches

This kitchen effortlessly combines a diverse range of materials, including stainless steel and marble, all against a light-colored backdrop of cabinetry.

68

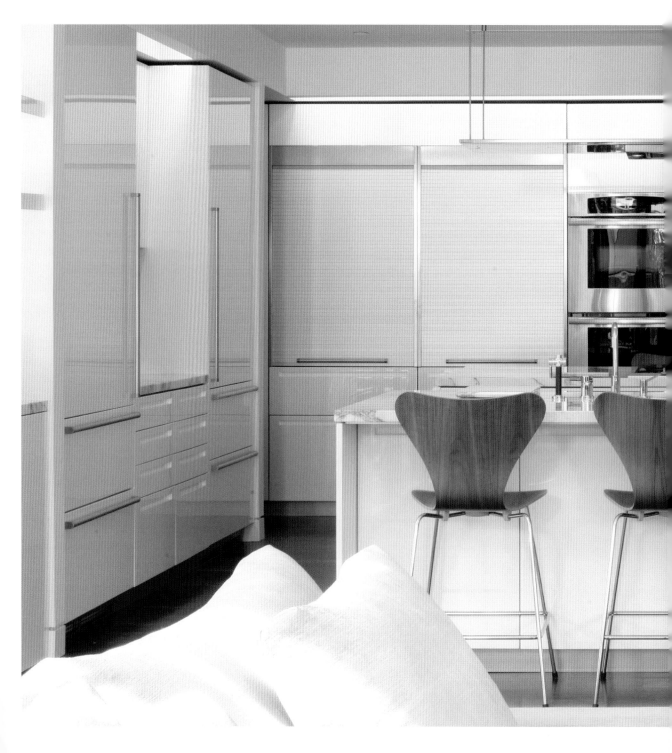

Here lighting serves as a visual separation of the kitchen and dining area, with artificial light giving way to natural light as you move through the space. The movable gray island easily adapts to both areas.

69

Here the long, white Corian table/countertop leading to the floor-to-ceiling window overlooking the Mediterranean Sea is reminiscent of a diving board, encouraging your eyes to leap toward the water.

70

The triangular attic space houses the simple kitchen, using up what could be considered "dead" space. The sloping walls contain small windows to provide natural light and ventilation.

71

Warm elements like the wooden
floorboards and table contrast
with the gray-blue kitchen
cabinetry, which is reminiscent
of the rocks found out in the
landscape beyond the windows.

72

73 The color black can exude a luxurious and glamorous air. Here, aluminum finishes accent the black. The clean, modular appearance is reminiscent of an office design, and the mix of dishes with books on the shelves supports this.

74

The curved forms found in this kitchen, including the cabinetry and sideboard, help soften the linear and industrial feel in the space. The work area features excellent flow and an ergonomic design.

75

The long island, which extends well past the wall it faces, is the core of this kitchen. Clean, white open storage areas are sandwiched between the light wood cabinets.

76

The thick column performs both esthetic and structural functions, supporting the polished wood platform. The wood surface can perform numerous jobs, acting as a countertop, work space or eating area.

77

The combination of clean stainless steel with precisely placed task lighting and choice of faucets with spray attachments give this kitchen a laboratory feel, just waiting for cooking "experiments."

This unit, with its futuristic design, evokes something you might find on a space shuttle. It is distinct but still practical, with the retractable top – complete with plants – opening up to reveal the stovetop and sink.

78

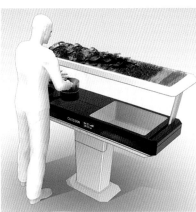

79 Thanks to a little ingenuity and adaptable technology, this kitchen appliance can go where you need it. Its height is adjustable, and it comes complete with wheels and three induction stovetop areas. Plus, when the stove is turned off, it can be used as a tabletop.

80

This kitchen offers a variety of
work spaces. Its highlight is the
cylindrical island, featuring a
cooktop, sink and effective
task lighting.

This simple but functional
kitchen is separated from the
rest of the space by a thin, black
marble wall. The stark white tray
attached to the marble serves as
a small, individual dining area.

81

An efficient kitchen is made not only through the overall kitchen design, but also in the finer details of storage areas. Here, specific storage was created for spices, knives and other kitchen tools and essentials.

82

83

The height of the room, accentuated by painting the walls black, evokes the feeling of a theater stage. The clean lines and contrast of the upper cabinetry against the black background almost makes them appear to float.

The centerpiece of this elegant,
monotone kitchen is the leather
and stainless steel range hood.
The opening in the partition wall
is purposely designed to view
this feature.

84

85

Using marble in the kitchen for the sink area countertop and backsplash is an innovative idea, as it's a material more often seen on bathroom vanities. The wood cabinetry and stainless steel handles complement the effect.

This kitchen was designed with the idea of working straight from the garden, with fresh food being prepped, processed, cooked and preserved or immediately eaten and enjoyed.

86

87

This kitchen features a variety of storage areas, including different cabinetry styles as well as both open and closed shelving. The rough porphyry countertop is the most alluring part of the room.

88 This well-divided and organized cabinet space dispels the idea that disorder may reign behind closed doors. The unit is mounted on a retractable frame, making good use of space that may be too high to access without a step stool.

The combination of dark wood
with stainless steel works well
in this linear kitchen. The glass
shelves with metal framing make
the dishes appear to float.

89

90

A range hood with built-in lighting provides the dual benefit of removing fumes as well as providing task lighting over the stove.

91 These revolving kitchens, measuring 20 square feet (1.8 sq. m), are ideal for small homes or offices. Despite their size, they have a lot to offer, including a stovetop, oven, sink, fan, dishwasher, storage and even a garbage can.

These wall-mounted, self-contained kitchen units can be opened up when needed or closed when kitchen work is done. The buyer can choose from a variety of features to include in each module, such as a stove, cooktop, microwave and different storage options.

92

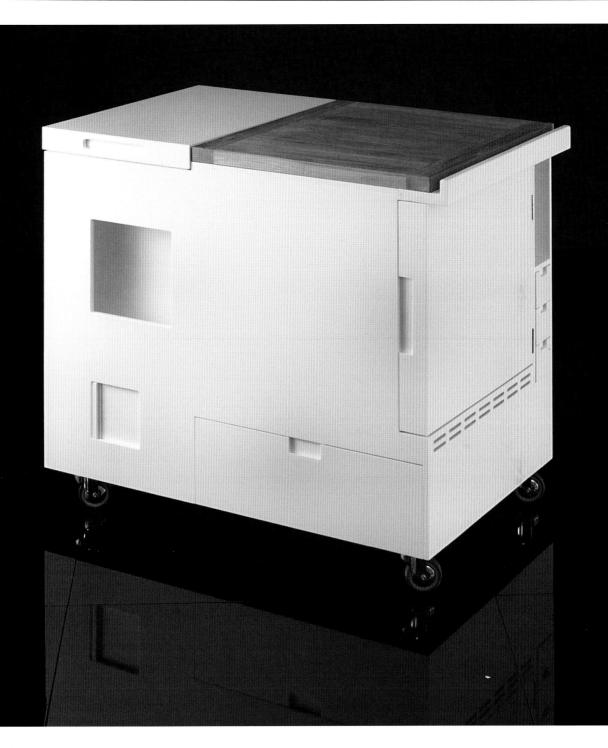

93

What's great about units with ample storage is that you can use whatever you need when you need it, and hide away the rest. This unit even incorporates drawers that can act as a table and two seats.

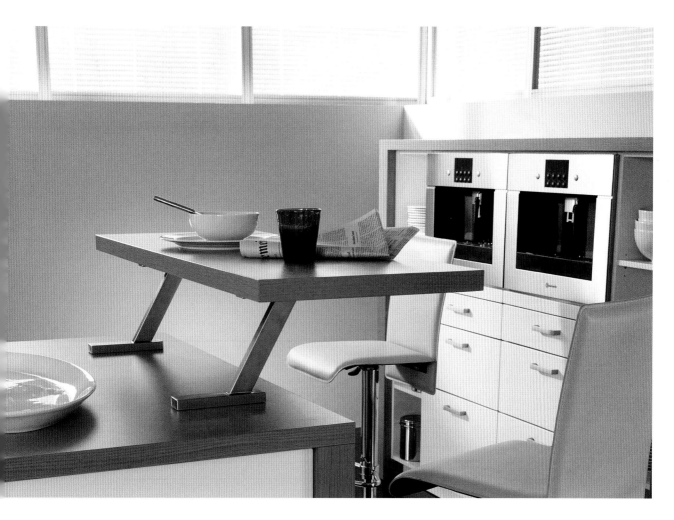

94

Clever, ergonomic designs
are seen more and more often
in the kitchen. Typically, the key
is to optimize the space, thus
combining practicality
and esthetics.

95

The addition of small surfaces, like this tray, generates a range of possibilities when organizing a space. It also adds interest to the room.

96

This predominantly white kitchen, complete with stark, simple lighting, contrasts with the choice of a smooth wood floor, which provides warmth to give the room a homey feel.

97

The brightness of the different white surfaces gives a gentle airiness to the room. The lines are simple, giving this kitchen a sense of visual purity.

98   The top part of this sphere houses the work area of the kitchen. When closed, the unit emits a dim light, complemented by the wall unit off to the side.

99 Monochromatic tones from brown to cream predominate in this open space area. Containing the kitchen, dining room and living room, the space feels warm and contemporary.

BATHROOMS

CERAMIC | CONCRETE | GLASS | MARBLE | PAINT AND WALLPAPER

STONE | WOOD | MISCELLANEOUS

CERAMIC

The use of ceramic in bathrooms has a long history. Baking the material at high temperatures gives it an extraordinary degree of hardness, making it highly efficient and resistant to wear, light, temperature extremes and chemicals. Ceramics are once again coming into their own, due to their elegance and practicality. There are a variety of surfaces and styles available, including glazed and stony looks, as well as different sizes, ranging from small mosaics to large tiles.

100

This bathroom is reminiscent of a Roman bath house, with small mosaic tiles in various shades of ocher and other tiles in earth tones. The metallic finish of the faucets and mirrors works well with the reflective quality of the tile.

101

The diagonal pattern of the floor tiles contrasts with the vertical wall tiles. The reflection of the prevailing colors of white and blue gives the room a very nautical feel.

102

This bathroom combines baroque and classical styles, creating a luxurious space without excessive ornamentation. The brown and white tiles are used to complement and highlight the decorative features.

103

The mosaic tiles on the wall, in a palette of pale blues, creates the illusion of being inside a swimming pool. This, combined with the white ceramic floor, ceiling and fixtures, creates a scene reminiscent of a Mediterranean landscape.

104

Green tones in this bathroom evoke feelings of nature. Aiding in the relaxing air of the room are the large, circular bathtub and a variety of rest areas.

105

The design of this bathroom, featuring a collage of tiles in different sizes, colors, direction, and textures, creates a space that is both modern and inviting. The predominance of green heightens the sense of freshness and tranquility.

Whether it is found on bathroom
floors, walls or fixtures, ceramic
offers an element of creativity.
Here, the combination of different
tiles creates an elegant, artistic
composition.

106

In this angular bathroom, the design provides an optimal balance between privacy and open concept. The ample amount of natural lighting prevents the room from becoming too dark and somber.

107

108 Here the floor and walls are covered with small tiles in shades of white and gray. The result is a light and clean design that works well with the minimalist elements in the room.

109 Tubing wrapped in wood veneer serves as an original structure for a full bathroom. Brown and white mosaic tiles, which match the color scheme of the tube, create a classic elegance.

110

The use of two-tone mosaic tiles creates elegant borders that give this bathroom a feel that is both classic and contemporary. The warm lighting and the sunken bathtub and shower enhance the feel of spaciousness.

111

The white fixtures, wall, and fabrics are greatly enhanced by the captivating lighting that bathes the ceramic and glass with a gleam and creates the impression that the faucets are jewels on display.

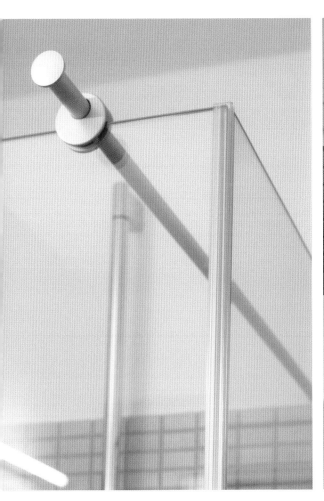

112

The use of uniform mosaic tiles on walls and floors provides continuity to the different surfaces and visually enlarges this small room. The long mirror and glass shower enclosure also allow light to flow through the space.

113

This bathroom, featuring an open-plan design and which is integrated in the master bedroom, acts as a striking stage, with its saturated colors, asymmetric wall sconces, rounded corners, exposed plumbing, and the distinct bathtub as its focal point.

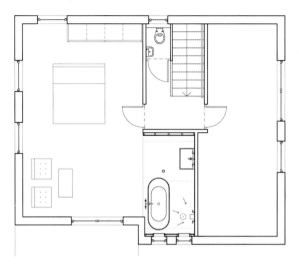

Floor Plan

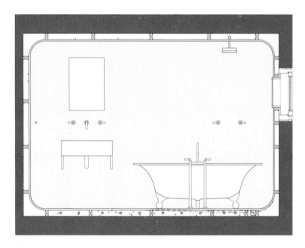

Section

Second floor plan

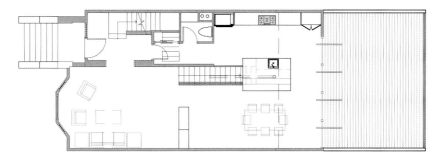

First floor plan

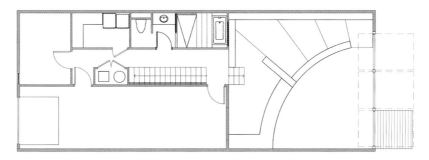

Basement floor plan

Ceramic tiles in warm pink tones cover most of the floor and walls, with bands of red highlighting the tub and sinks. This choice of color allows the white fixtures, which resemble pottery, to pop.

114

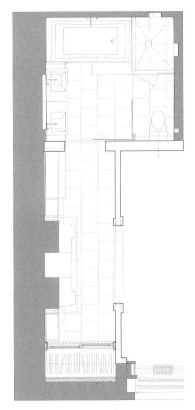

Floor plan

115

This bathroom is the epitome of formal eclecticism. Diverse materials, including fabric, ceramic and wood, as well as a variety of colors and recessed lights work together and also help delineate the different areas of the room.

116

The dark shade of the mosaic tiles, as well as their rich and refined feel, creates a sensuous ambience in this bathroom. The colors continue into the adjoining bedroom, creating a cohesive design.

The use of mosaic tiles in the bathroom offers an endless range of design possibilities. This bathroom does not require any flourishes of decor, as the tiles are inherently decorative on their own.

117

118   Ceramic is commonly used for sinks, and while their design can be simplistic, it can also be practical with additional details. This sink also features a shelf, vanity top and towel holder.

119

The focal point of this predominantly gray and white bathroom is the red tiled tub surround. The bathtub rests in its base, with a small ledge running around for support.

120

Dominated by clean lines, the different tones of white in this bathroom separate the different surfaces and features from one another. The lighting helps to open up and brighten the space further.

Floor plan

CONCRETE

In bathrooms, concrete can provide a strong and modern feel. Its industrial connotation fits nicely into urban-style homes, but it can be equally attractive in rural households, with their plain and elemental spirit.
The durability and resistance of concrete is indisputable. Cleaning is a simple task, so it is undoubtedly practical.
It also allows for an eye-catching contrast with other materials, be they natural or artificial.

121

This long, gray concrete countertop exudes a sense of strength. It runs parallel to the floor, which is made of the same material, and stands out against the pure white walls.

122

The light-colored walls and lighting over the fixtures create the impression that the concrete bases might almost be shadows in this bathroom. The subtle tones create a simple contrast.

123

Huge floor to ceiling windows let sunlight into a space where concrete is the dominant feature. Its presence on the floor, ceiling and walls turns the room into a kind of natural cave and creates a lively, inviting and cool space.

Red bathroom sections

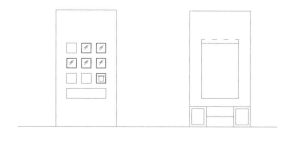

Black bathroom plans

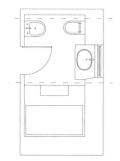

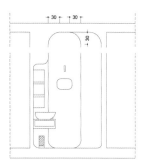

White bathroom section

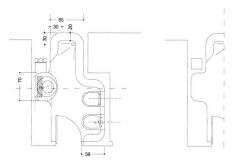

White bathroom plan

124 Concrete is used throughout this bathroom to eye-popping effect. Recesses in the wall act as shelving, while a large recess in one of the base pieces serves as a bathtub.

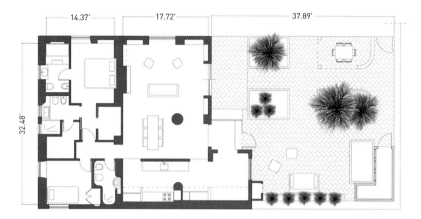

Before renovation plan

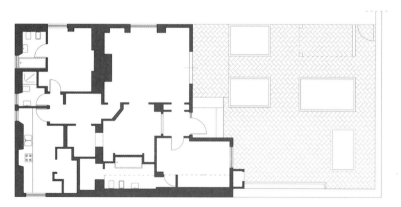

After renovation plan

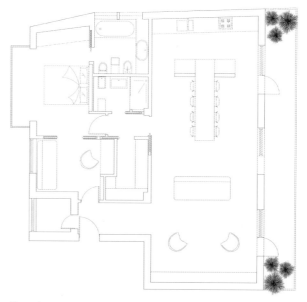

Floor plan

Black concrete creates an
intimate feel in this bathroom.
The recessed lighting focuses
light on the ceramic fixtures,
which almost appear to float in
the room.

125

This bathroom is connected to the bedroom by a glass wall, creating a space that feels both solid and open. The room is very angular, giving the room a very linear and almost "cubist" feel.

126

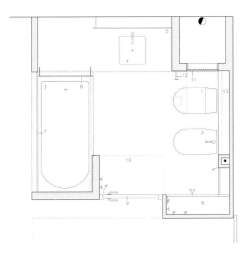

Master bathroom plan

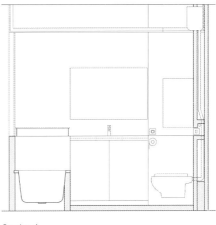

Section A

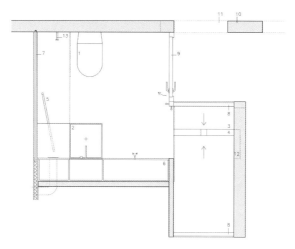

Small bathroom plan

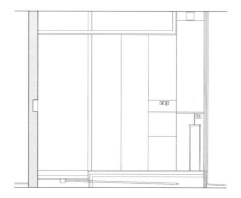

Section D

The clean, unencumbered lines of this simple sink counter the heavy feel of the concrete floor. The indirect lighting, reflective surfaces and delicate towel holder add lightness to the space.

127

128

The palette of warm, earthy colors in this bathroom is complemented by the rough texture of the distinct concrete wall. The horizontal bands of different thicknesses emphasize the handcrafted and personal nature of the work that went into it.

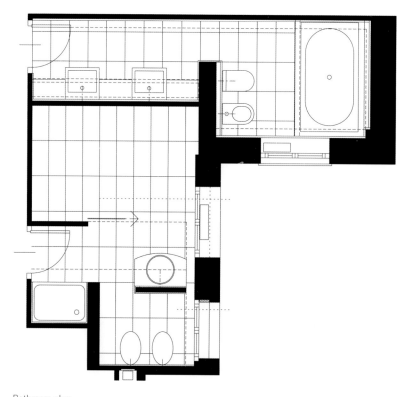

Bathroom plan

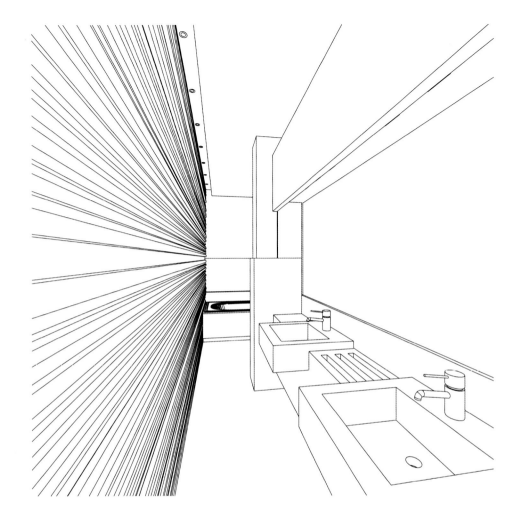

129

The series of bands on the concrete wall is reflected in the huge mirror that crowns the entire length of the vanity top: a design feature that creates the impression that this grooved texture fully surrounds the room.

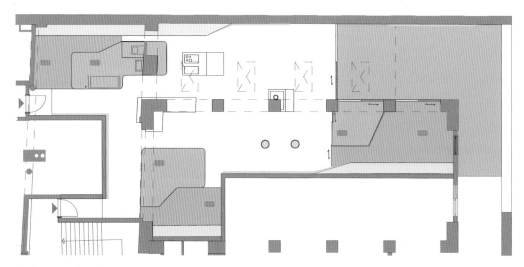

Before renovation plan

The open plan of a former
factory is preserved in this loft,
and the bathroom provides a
fresh, invigorating atmosphere.
The strength of the cement
contrasts with the softer
translucent surfaces.

130

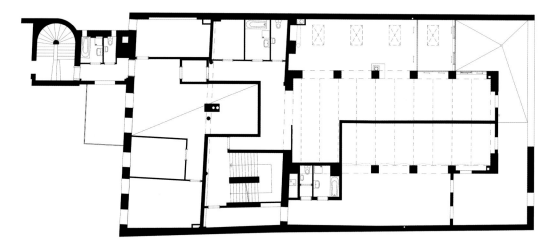

After renovation plan

The cement backdrop of this bathroom gives a genuine, almost industrial feel to the room. However, the polished wood, sunken basin sink and minimalist wall-mount faucet lend an air of elegance.

131

GLASS

The use of glass in bathrooms can overcome the traditional sense of enclosure found there while stil providing privacy.

Glass gives a feeling of airiness and weightlessness, as well as timeless elegance. It can be used in walls as well as enclosures, sinks, closets and shelves. In addition to clear glass, frosted and colored glass can be used to great effect.

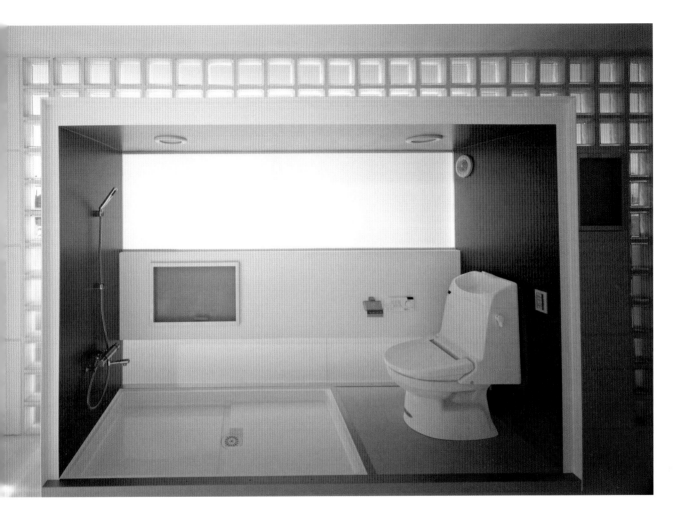

132

In this distinct bathroom, elements are kept to a minimum, with a toilet and a shower. Colored glass allows diffused light to enter from the side.

133

Adjustable downlighting provides all the light for this bathroom. Reflective surfaces, including the large glass shower enclosure, white marble and cabinet mirrors, aid in giving the room an open feel.

134

This bathroom was designed with relaxation in mind, as seen in the reclining lounge chair and soothing color choices. The vessel sink, sauna-looking wood and clear shower enclosure work well with this theme.

135

The combination of window sizes, patterned fabrics, glass decor and mirrors with the light tones of the walls, vanity and fixtures, create a soft, ethereal feel in this bathroom.

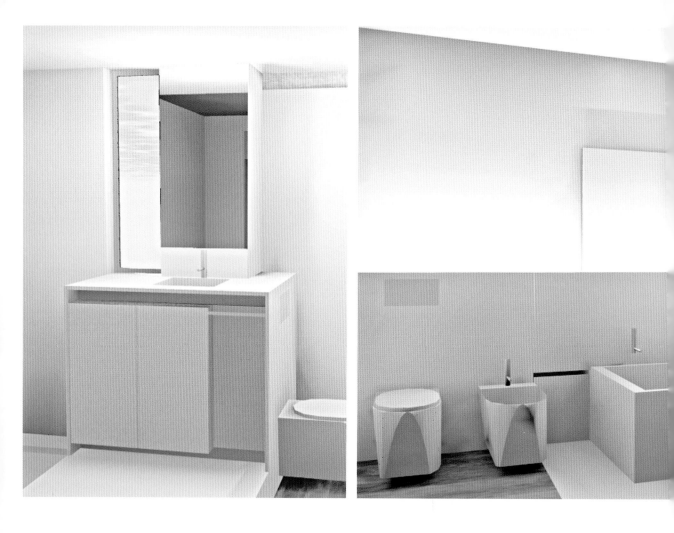

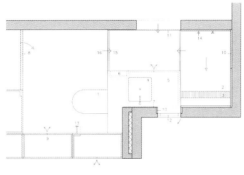

Small bathroom floor plan

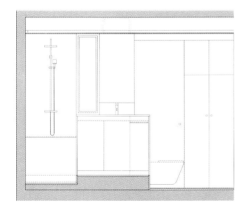

Section A

Section B

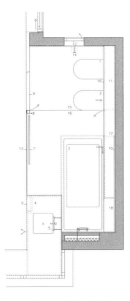

Ground floor ensuite bathroom

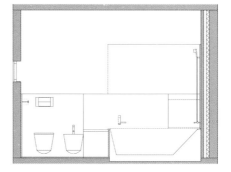

Section B

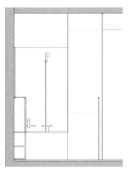

Section C

Here, glass plays a starring role against traditional opaque walls. The varied glass surfaces connect the spaces, providing light, reflection and added luminosity.

136

137

Clean glass surfaces, devoid of trim or other edging, easily blend into a space and create fluidity. In spaces with predominantly neutral colors, glass can define an entrance without creating a break in flow and continuity.

138

The focal point of this bathroom is the glass shower wall, affixed only to the floor, which can work well in bathrooms with limited space for a shower. Its simplicity complements the clean lines of the shower unit and rainspout shower head.

139

An effective way to give surfaces a gleaming finish is to line them with glass. The distinct reflection of the room's features in the walls provides a unique design, giving the room a watery feel.

This room uses glass, mirror, white fixtures and light to create a bright, elegant space. The effect is harmonious, and makes the bathroom feel large, open and airy.

140

When working with neutral walls, adding glass features like a vanity, sinks and shelving, creates a lightweight feel in the room and gives it a sense of purity. Wall-mount faucets accentuate the minimalism and clean lines.

141

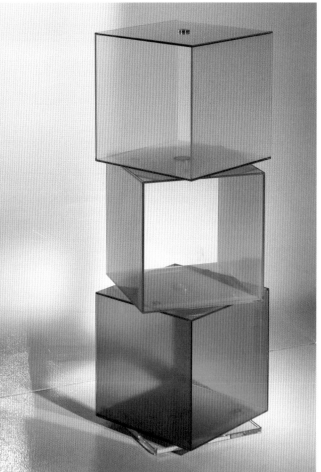

MARBLE

In essence, marble provides a sense of nobility and elegance in any space, and it is increasingly found in bathrooms. Depending on the pattern and coloration found in the marble, it can be used to create effects ranging from traditional to modern, and simply elegant to ostentatious.

142

Rooms tiled with marble nearly always provide a luxurious atmosphere. Here, the rounded lines found in the sink, toilet and tub work well with the marble surround.

143

A palette of pinks and soft beiges covering all the surfaces of a bathroom harks back to the splendor of ancient times. Details such as the painting on the wall, the striated column and the mirror frame provide the finishing touches for this classical ambience.

144

Marble in the vanity, lower walls and flooring serve to ground this room. The wood in the vanity and the upper walls contrasts with the smooth, shiny marble and gives the room added warmth.

145

The detailed textures found on the ceilings and floors, combined with varied rustic decor and plants, provide a relaxing, elegant feel in this bathroom. The brocatelle marble on the tub ledge gives the room an added hint of glamor.

146

The large marble tiles in different shades give a sense of solidity to the floor and walls. Frameless, inset mirrors reflect the pattern of the tiles and provide a clean, linear look in the room.

The luxurious marble floor with its delicate curved pattern is a perfect complement to the antique-styled furniture. The highlighted features in this space are the bathtub and shower, which are covered in more heavily patterned marble tiles.

147

148

The toilet, bidet, shower enclosure and tub are found on the perimeter of this bathroom, raised up and separated from the center of the room by a strip of black marble. The floor is decorated with moderate marble tiles, while the walls carry large marble slabs.

149

When seen from the bedroom, this relaxing and inviting bathroom almost seems like it could be a large photomural on the wall. The bathtub is a focal point, with the amber light drawing your eye into the room.

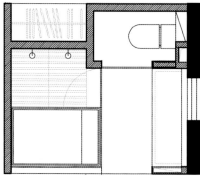

Before design plan

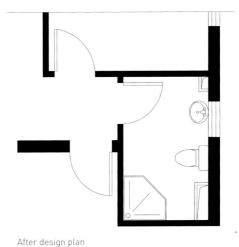

After design plan

150

The white bathtub glows thanks to the lit base, an effect even more pronounced when contrasted with the darkened bedroom. The shower is given a simpler, less noticeable place in the room.

151

The veins on the white marble that covers the entire bathroom, except for the ceiling, could almost be brush strokes purposefully added to bring the room to life. The glass shower enclosure and the mirror increase the sense of light in the space.

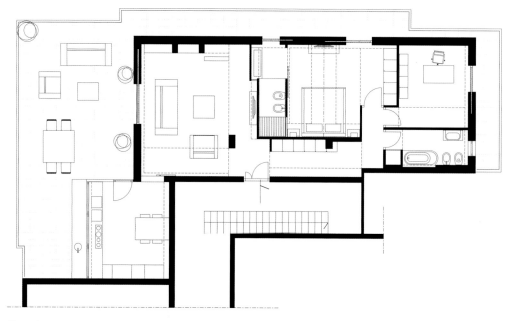

Floor plan

This bathroom is connected to
the master bedroom by a sliding
wood door, and by the continuity
of the light colors on the walls of
both rooms. The predominance
of marble on the bathroom walls
is dazzling.

152

153

The heavily patterned marble on the vanity top and walls in this bathroom are striking and almost animal-like, and they give the surfaces a sense of movement. In contrast, the white sink and tub seem still, grounded and motionless.

PAINT AND WALLPAPER

Painted or wallpapered surfaces offer a nearly endless range of design possibilities, as well as functional practicality, as they provide a washable, durable surface.
Making the correct choice in colors and patterns can complement the other elements and motifs in the room.

154

The different textures, colors and shapes in this bathroom combine to create a fun, whimsical space. Bright colors in the cabinetry, light fixtures and bathtub pop agains the neutral gray walls.

155

The armchair, mirror, chandelier and bathtub lend a very decadent air to this bathroom. The golden tones found in all these accents are also seen in the dense, striped wallpaper.

156

The soft pastel color of the wall contrasts with the hard, brown wood furniture. A strip of mirror along the cabinets and the rounded tub both soften the look of the backdrop.

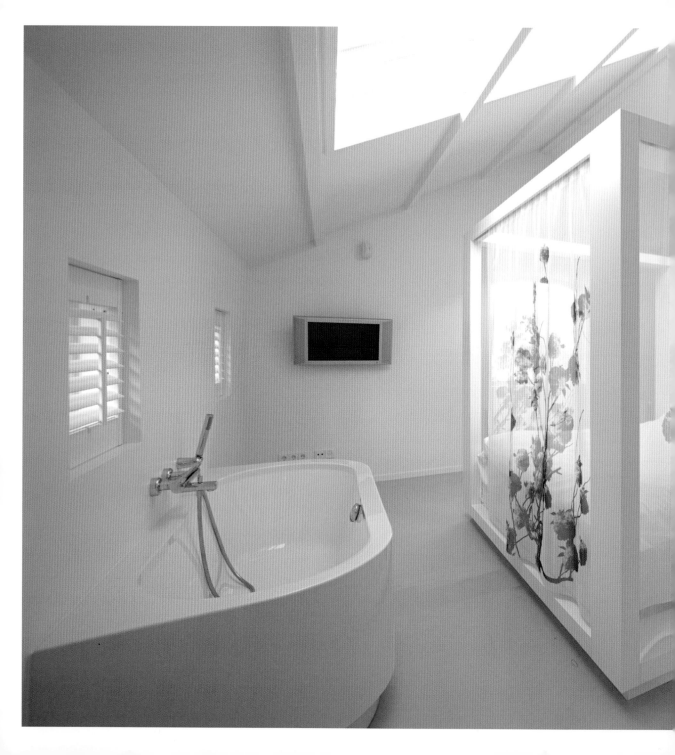

157

Here, the bedroom and bathroom are adjoined, barely separated from one another. The whiteness of the room is only disturbed by the floral print on the curtain. The curved bathtub is a highlight in the room, while the simple shower remains hidden.

158

Simple white walls, flooring and accents are the perfect backdrop for a few dark, shadowy highlights and create a glamorous feel reminiscent of the 1930s. Every object here is a purposely placed work of art, giving the room an almost museumlike quality.

STONE

Some people call stone the younger brother of marble. Nevertheless, its versatility allows for a wide range of design ideas.

Because of its natural origins, stone walls come in a variety of shades and textures. Depending on the style to be achieved, these aspects can be balanced along with the size of the slabs to create different effects. It is particularly well combined with wood elements in the room.

159

Lime green fills a bathroom that crosses the line between simple and extravagant. Different linear surfaces combine to create a clean and energetic feel.

160

Rough reddish stone with an aged appearance covers the walls and floor in this bathroom, giving the space a strong personality. The metallic panels break the monotony and provide an urban, contemporary feel.

161

Here, space in the basement was used to combine a sauna, bathroom and laundry area. The black granite wall separates the bathtub on the one side from the sink on the other.

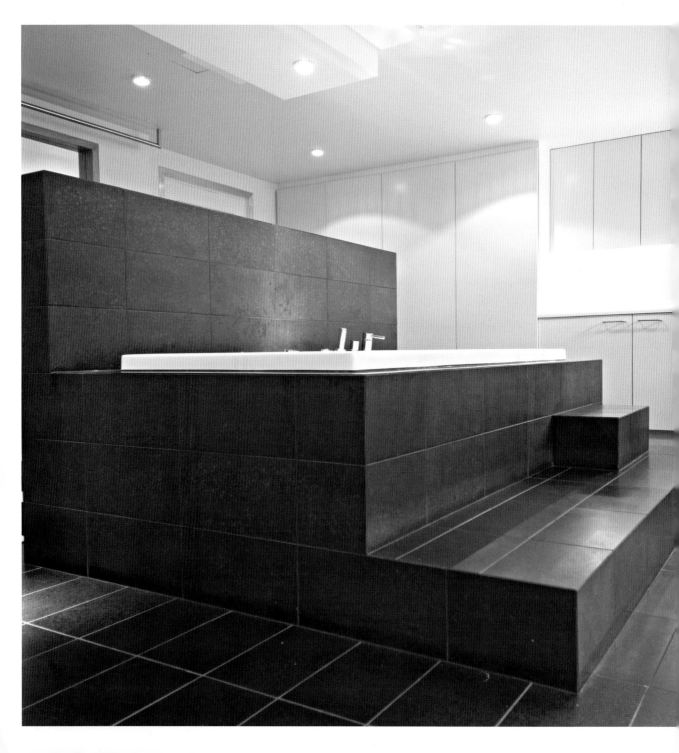

Granite, glass and oak are combined in this bathroom to great effect. Strategically placed wall sconces provide lighting that gives a relaxed feel to a modern take on an ancient Roman bath.

162

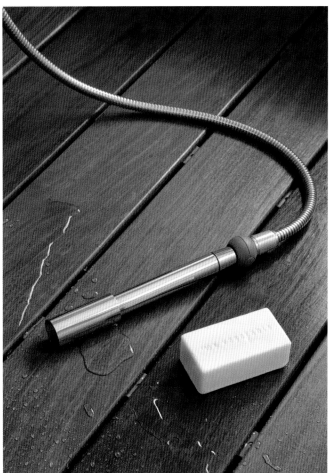

163   The combination of different stone surfaces - exquisitely polished and roughly textured - works well in this bathroom, giving it the feel of a subterranean spa.

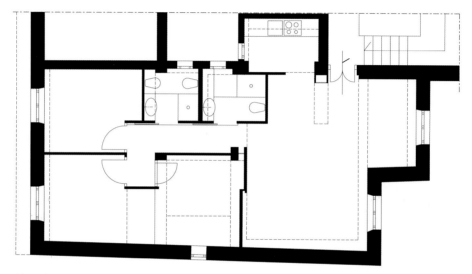

Floor plan

Retaining the industrial slate on the vanity tops and floors creates continuity in the bathrooms in this home. Clean white fixtures create a refreshing, crisp effect against the black.

164

165

A multitude of details, including arched windows, glass block wall, traditional cabinetry and candles give this space an almost religious feel. The small, refined bathtub is placed near the center of the room.

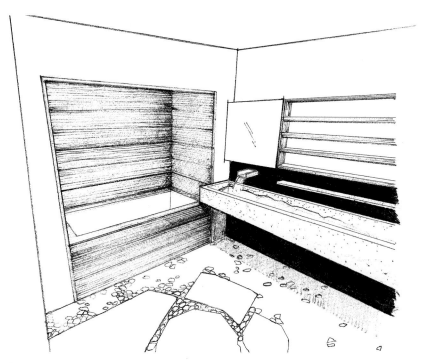

Sketch

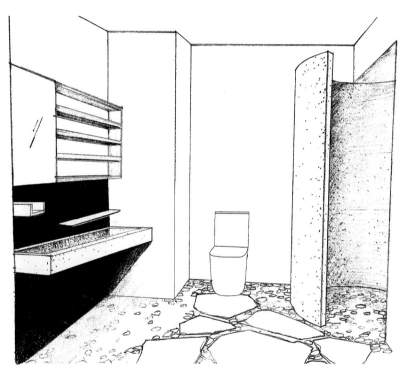

Sketch

This room conbines the features
of a traditional Japanese bath
house. Despite the mixture of
textures and tones, the spirit of
craftsmanship, attention to detail
and the serenity of unadulterated
nature predominate.

166

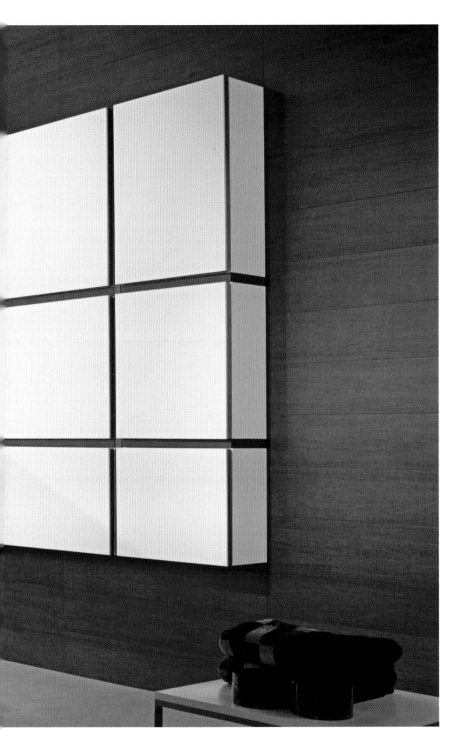

167

The striking feature of this bathroom is its thick and solemn walls that provide a strong backdrop to the room. White modular cabinets and an inverted triangular sink contrast and complement the angular nature of the room.

Only the addition of sinks and a tub define this area as a bathroom, as its decor does not feel like a traditional bathroom space. The potlights, dark panels and large gray tiles create a modern, monochromatic space that could be found elsewhere in the home.

168

WOOD

Wood is renowned for its warmth, making it a particularly popular material for some of our most treasured and loved pieces of furniture.

In addition to other parts of the home, wood has a place in the bathroom. Polished or rough, knotted or smooth, dark or light, boarded or planked, it is a natural material that can give almost anything that feel of furniture, especially if it possesses the richness of oak or cherry.

169

It's easy to have a soothing soak in this bathroom with the serene view out the window and the wood platform and ledge of the tub. Wood is also used here in the ceiling beams, flooring and vanity top.

170

The floor of this bathroom is decked out with polished wood floorboards. There are more stripes on the wall in the grooved finish. The solidity and neutrality of the large white bathtub breaks up the pattern.

171

This bathroom commands an excellent view and takes full advantage of natural light to enhance the pale walls, clear glass and mid-grained wood color. The tub occupies a prestigious place in the way it is elevated and positioned close to the windows.

172

Wood inside this bathroom blends harmoniously with the waterfront and wood decking seen beyond the glass. Here, the bathtub is placed right next to the window, while the sink and toilet are positioned further back in the room.

173

The bedroom and bathroom are enmeshed in this space. The toilet and shower are hidden from view, but the vanity is positioned next to the bed and the bathtub offers a soak with a waterfront view, as it rests next to the windows.

174

The use of wood in a bathroom is traditionally limited to shelving and cabinetry. Here it is used in that way, as well as to frame the bathtub and as the vanity top.

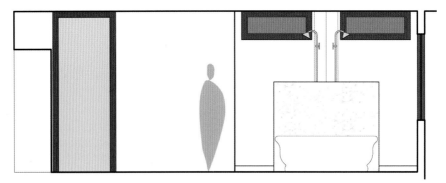

Elevation

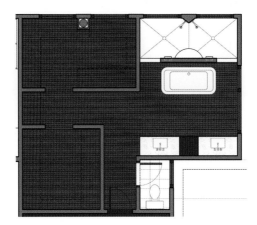

Master bathroom plan

175

Following the design of the rest of this home, the bathroom is predominantly wood - even up to the stepped ceiling. If not for the view of lush woodland through the windows, you might think this bathroom is in a ship's cabin.

176

Bathrooms can be places of comfort and relaxation, but practicality is important. This bathroom is separated from the closet by a mirrored wall that reflects the view out the window.

177

Lighting filtered through a fabric lampshade heightens the sense of subdued relaxation in this bathroom. Polished wood, marble and the clean white of the sink and bathtub create an inviting atmosphere.

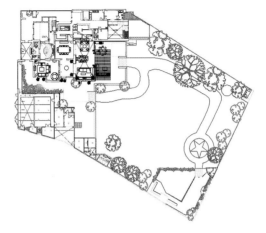

Ground floor plan

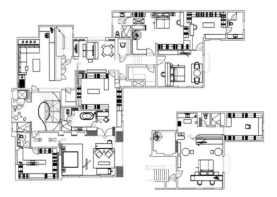

Second floor plan

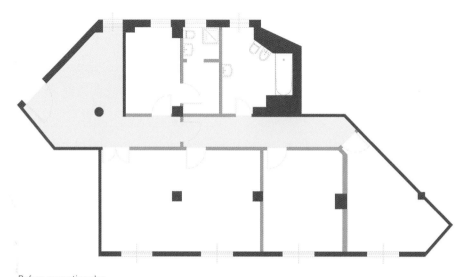

Before renovation plan

Installing a new wood floor in a bathroom is often enough to change its personality and add warmth and refinement. Here the small, raised deck in the shower adds interest, and the red column gives an urban feel to the space.

178

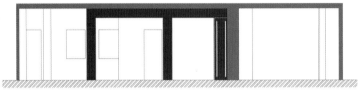

Section

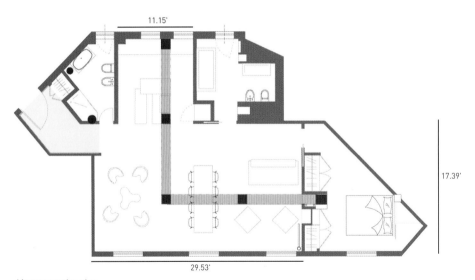

After renovation plan

179

The space has been filled with wooden cabinetry and shelves, which act as effective storage. The light teak floors are a continuation from the rest of the house. The sink juts out from the vanity, as if it wants to attract attention.

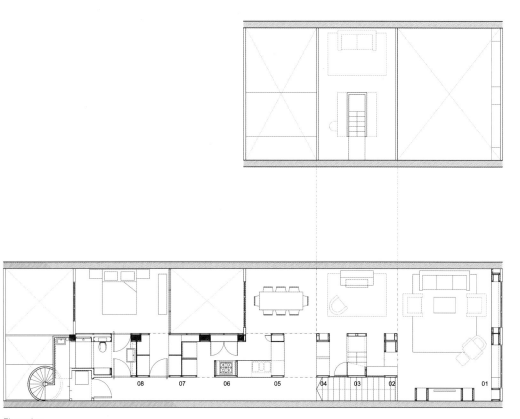

Floor plan

180

This bathroom features textured materials in calming, subdued colors. The defined wood framing makes a strong statement against the soft hues and transparent glass surfaces.

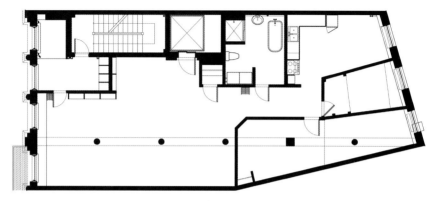

Before renovation plan

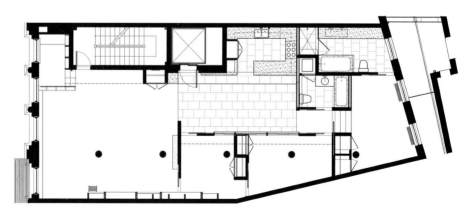

After renovation plan

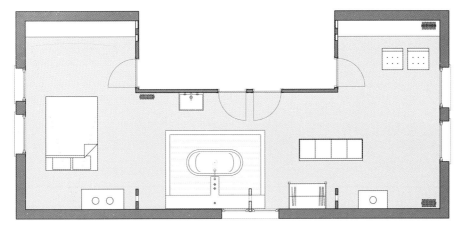

Floor plan

181

181

This attic was redesigned and renovated to make the elements of everyday life special. The bathroom is located at the center of the room, between the closet and bedroom. Its placement on a platform makes it even more of a standout feature.

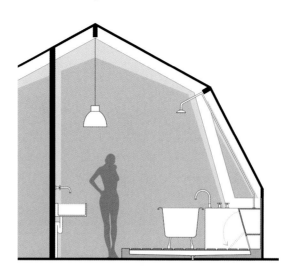

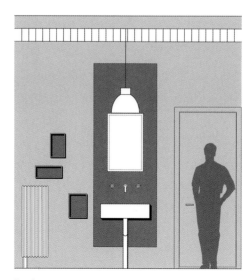

Sections

182 Wood strips cover most surfaces of this room, akin to a miniature dollhouse made with matchsticks. The space is a harmonious blend of old, new, rustic and contemporary styles.

183

Here, wood is used in a very unlikely place, as the seats for the toilet and bidet. The wood provides a warm support surface, and nicely contrasts with the ultra-sanitary metal bowl.

The standalone bathtub sets the mood of this bathroom. With its predominant size and cedar finish, it's reminiscent of a giant bowl. The simple faucet keeps the look clean and simple.

184

MISCELLANEOUS

As with any other room in the house, the bathroom can invoke the imagination of everyone who uses it. It can be a highlight of the home, not merely a necessary space. Chandeliers, columns, art and luxurious fabrics can all be found here.

As well, essential items like sinks and bathtubs can extend beyond their function into ornamental and artistic forms, and act as focal points in the space.

185

A neutral color scheme allows the possibility of bringing in decor and fabrics that infuse life into the space. Here, ornamental details include the faucets and clawfoot bathtub.

186

Every inch of this bathroom exudes luxury and glamor. In addition to the marble floors and vanity, the wooden cabinetry, refined faucets and lighting, crystal knobs and gleaming metallic bathtub add splendor.

187

The mixture of stone, ceramic and different wood finishes make for a bathroom with a rustic feel but which is undeniably innovative. The neutral colors blend together, working well in the overall design.

188

The impetuous color scheme of this room, with a palette that includes ochers, browns, greens and yellows, is reminiscent of an Impressionist painting. The lighting and reflections, together with the grass, bamboo and vase, evoke a distinct Oriental ambience.

189

The heaviness of the stone is counteracted by the curving walls and shower door, as well as the ceramic floor tiles. The earthy feel of this bathroom is brightened by the abundant lighting and large vanity mirror.

190

The exquisite marble on the floor and parts of the wall produces a luxurious, radiant effect in this bathroom. The soft diffused lighting intensifies the warm, decadent feel of the room.

191

This attic bathroom, limited in space, is used to best advantage with the prime features of sink and tub placed on the diagonal. Lighting is provided by a lamp near the corner and skylights overhead.

192

This curved, asymmetrical bathtub is the focal point of the room. It rests on a tiled platform with matching tiled wall that also contains the glass-walled shower.

When space is not a problem, it's possible to create a bathroom with all the luxury of a full suite. Here the drapery hanging over the large windows are reminiscent of stage curtains. At center, the bathtub rests on a platform, resembling a podium.

193

194   The various metal elements found in this bathroom – faucets, handles and light fixtures – almost float over the smoothness of the marble, white wood and glass. The whole room is light and airy, and the windows in the shower enclosure add interest.

The white walls, floor and fixtures
in this bathroom act as a neutral
backdrop to the lush plant life.
The decor is an eclectic mix of
new and old materials, blended
together in a cohesive style.

195

196

The shiny, refined faucets stand out against the resin and polyester bathtub and sink. These fixtures, manufactured with handles at the ends that double as towel holders, are reminiscent of old washbowls.

The plants and diffused lighting
soften the boundaries in this
room, and gel nicely with
influences from traditional
Japanese art. The decorative
ornamentation is ample, but feels
lightweight and emits a sense of
tranquility in the room.

197

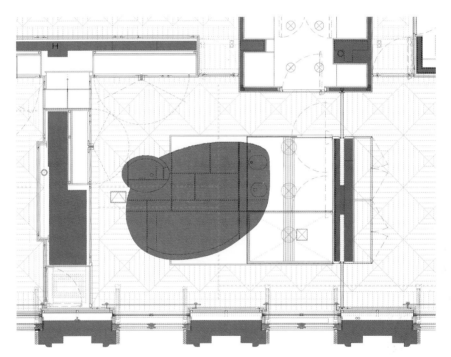

Master bathroom plan

198

This golden feature piece contains the sink and bathtub, as well as a toilet on the other side of the glass. Recessed lights in the ceiling illuminate it as if it was a jewel. The adjoining shower is tucked away and more neutral by comparison.

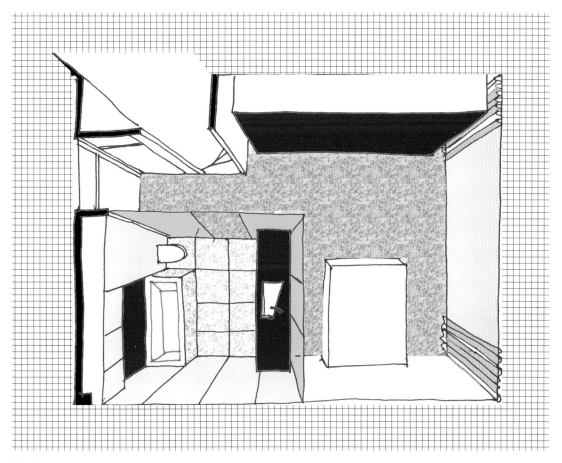

Sketch

199

Emerald green surrounds this bathroom through actual green surfaces as well as reflected areas. Glass panels allow privacy and give a pleasing ambience, even in half-light.

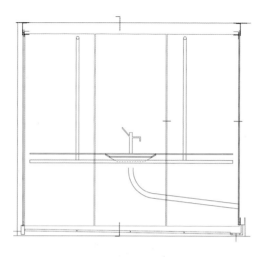

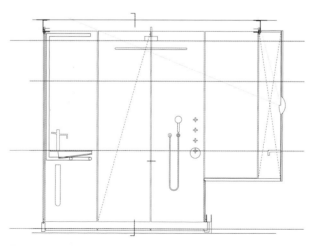

Sections

200

A slender bathtub rests on a brocatelle marble floor with coloration reminiscent of sea foam. The iridescent mosaic tiles evoke the sense of sky meeting sea. A bright fuchsia armchair creates a place to enjoy the view.

DIRECTORY

Markus Wespi Jérôme de Meuron Architekten
www.wespidemeuron.ch
© Hannes Henz
p. 174-175, 252-255

Matali Crasset
www.matalicrasset.com
© Uwe Spoering
p. 522-523, 599

MGS Designs
www.mgstaps.com
© MGS Designs
p. 124 left, 126

Michele Saee
www.michelesaee.com
© Chensu
p. 30

Miró Rivera Architects
www.mirorivera.com
© Paul Finkel
p. 236-239, 682-687

Mobalco
www.mobalco.com
© Mobalco
p. 56-57, 330

MoHen Design
www.mohen-design.com
© MoHen Design
p. 572-579, 592, 642-643

Murdock Young Architects
www.murdockyoung.com
© Frank Oudeman
p. 256-258

Nadejda Topouzanov and Vladimir Topouzanov
www.sbt.qc.ca
© Vladimir Topouzanov
p. 142-147

One Plus Partnership
www.onepluspartnership.com
© Gabriel Leung
p. 432-439, 518, 544-545, 612-617, 641

Oonagh Ryan
www.oonaghryan.com
© Scott Mayoral, Oonagh Ryan, Stuart Gow
p. 240-245

Patricia Urquiola
www.patriciaurquiola.com
© Axor
p.762-767, 770-771

Paul Cha
www.paulchaarchitect.com
© Paul Cha
p. 710-714

Pierre Hebbelinck, Marie-Françoise Plissart
www.pierrehebbelinck.net
© Marie-Françoise Plissart
p. 68-71

Plystudio
www.ply-studio.com
© Stzernstudio
p. 702-707

Porcelanosa
www.porcelanosa.com
© Porcelanosa
p. 656-657

Project Orange
www.projectorange.com
© Gareth Gardner
p. 580-585

Rapsel
www.rapsel.it
© Rapsel
p. 474, 510 left , 547, 549, 722, 723 right

Rational
www.rational.de
© Rational
p. 60-61, 288-289, 334-335, 354-357

RB Arkitektur
www.rbarkitektur.se
© RB Arkitektur
p. 634-639

Rekker System / Jordi López & Sergi Comellas
www.rekkersystem.com
© Rekker System
p. 378-385

Regia
www.regia.it
© Regia
p. 524

Rieber
www.rieber.de
© Rieber
p. 127

Santman van Staaden architecten
www.santman.nl
© Paul Santman
p. 786-791

Scape Architects
www.scapeestudio.com
© Kilian O'Sullivan
p. 309-311

Scavolini
www.scavolini.es
© Scavolini
p. 116, 117, 324-325

Schiffini
www.schiffini.it
© Schiffini
p. 82, 112, 350-351

Sheer
www.sheer.it
© Sheer
p. 386-387

Shutterstock
www.shutterstock.com
© Ajay Bhaskar | Shutterstock.com
p. 754
© Angelo Sarnacchiaro | Shutterstock.com
p. 397, 455
© archidea | Shutterstock.com
p. 600-601
© casadaphoto | Shutterstock.com
p. 570-571
© Debra James | Shutterstock.com
p. 755
© Dumitrescu Ciprian-Florin |
Shutterstock.com
p. 422
© gh19 | Shutterstock.com
p. 430, 662-663
© haveseen | Shutterstock.com
p. 489
© Henrik Winther Andersen |
Shutterstock.com
p. 396
© Inhabitant | Shutterstock.com
p. 598
© Koksharov Dmitry | Shutterstock.com
p. 394, 454, 756-757
© LuckyPhoto | Shutterstock.com
p. 569
© Maknt | Shutterstock.com
p. 602-603
© Maksym Bondarchuk | Shutterstock.com
p. 490-491
© Melanie DeFazio | Shutterstock.com
p. 559
© nsm | Shutterstock.com
p. 566-567
© Oleg - F | Shutterstock.com
p. 425
© Olemac | Shutterstock.com
p. 423

© Paul Matthew Photography |
Shutterstock.com
p. 647
© photobank.ch | Shutterstock.com
p. 631, 726
© photosphobos | Shutterstock.com
p. 560-561
© pics721 | Shutterstock.com
p. 550, 568, 732-733, 735, 758-761
© Rade Kovac | Shutterstock.com
p. 752-753
© roseburn3Dstudio | Shutterstock.com
p. 488, 661, 739
© Sergey Ostroukh | Shutterstock.com
p. 420-421
© Sklep Spozywczy | Shutterstock.com
p. 751
© Tomasz Markowski | Shutterstock.com
p. 399, 665
© Vadym Andrushchenko | Shutterstock.com
p. 453, 658
© Victoria Andreas | Shutterstock.com
p. 406-407
© yampi | Shutterstock.com
p. 792-793
© yuyangc | Shutterstock.com
p. 542-543, 597

Sicis
www.sicis.it
© Sicis
p. 440, 463, 511

Spg Architects
www.spgarchitects.com
© Spg Architects
p. 456-457

Stephen Jolson Architects
www.jolson.com.au
© Shania Shegedyn
p. 278

Swartz Design Associates
www.swartzdesign.com
© Swartz Design Associates
p. 87

Takao Shiotsuka Atelier
www.shio-atl.com
© Kaori Ichikawa
p. 284-287

Tow Studios Architecture
www.towarchitecture.com
© Eric Piasecki, Howard Tsao
p. 648-653

Valcucine
www.valcucine.it
© Valcucine
p. 100 left, 344-345, 348-349

Víctor Cañas
www.victor.canas.co.cr
© Jordi Miralles
p. 476-485

Villeroy & Boch
www.villeroy-boch.com
© Villeroy & Boch
p. 441

Vitra
www.vitra.com
© Vitra
p. 475

Zecc Architects
www.zecc.nl
© Cornbreadworks, Zecc Architetcts
p. 214-217